Sign Design Guide

a guide to inclusive signage

sponsored by

NOVA POLYMERS

Sign Design Guide

a guide to inclusive signage

Published in the United Kingdom by
JMU Access Partnership
224 Great Portland Street
London W1N 6AA

Sign Design Society
66 Derwent Road
Kinsbourne Green
Harpenden
Hertfordshire AL5 3NX

Sponsored by
Nova Polymers
27 Holywell Road
London EC2A 4JB

Authors*:	Peter Barker and June Fraser
Editor:	Tessa Palfreyman BSc (Eng)
Design and production:	June Fraser ARCA PPCSD
Illustrator:	Mark Booth BA (Hons)

*with additional contributions by:
Rachel Dalgleish, Sarah Hill,
Yvonne Howard and Mark Rose

Printed by
Offset Colour Print
159–179 Empress Road
Southampton SO2 0JW

ISBN 185878 412 3

Peter Barker and June Fraser

Sign Design Guide

a guide to inclusive signage

JMU and the Sign Design Society

Foreward by the Sponsors

Dear Professional

Nova Polymers are pleased to support JMU and the Sign Design Society in compiling the 'Sign Design Guide'. This Guide provides clear and concise information for the design and implementation of successful sign solutions which meet the requirements of the Disability Discrimination Act.

Nova Polymers believe this Guide shows how it is possible, by clear and concise guidelines, to design and specify signs that enhance the aesthetic appearance of building projects.

Nova Polymers products have been designed to allow the ideal Braille and embossed sign solution. We also recognise the need for design input and, as a result, we have built in all the design requirements for the modern building user – from paper based inserts to curved face signs. As well as being unique by offering incredible flexibility for sign design, the products also retain the all-important economic edge. This added design flexibility enables all sectors of commerce and industry to portray their corporate image, or identity, whilst maintaining DDA compliance.

Nova Polymers products were designed specifically for the American with Disabilities Act (ADA) in the United States where Braille and raised graphic signs have been a legal requirement for the past 8 years. The product is renowned for being one of the most sophisticated systems in the world for the production of this type of sign for visually impaired people.

We are confident that this manual gives the necessary information for designing the correct sign solution to meet DDA regulations. This will help visually impaired people to use the services of a company, or an institution, in an unaided and confident manner which is, after all, the ultimate goal.

Nova Polymers

> "70-75 per cent of the information we receive is given through eyesight. Anyone with a significant degree of sight loss, or no sight at all, will experience an 'information deficit'. So it is crucial that sign practitioners maximise the visibility and legibility of signs to make use of any remaining vision. Embossed, Braille and audible signs can improve access for those with limited vision."

Peter Barker, Manager, JMU

> "There are four basic principles in sign design:
> – signs should be used only when necessary
> – sign location should be part of the process of planning the building and the environment
> – messages should be short, simple and easily understood
> – signs should be consistent, using prescribed typefaces, colours and contrast."

June Fraser, Sign Design Society

Contents

Introduction

The 'Sign Design Guide' is a joint venture between JMU and the Sign Design Society (SDS). The intention is to set guidelines for good practice in sign design throughout the industry which will enable everyone, including visually impaired people, to have better access to information for wayfinding and orientation.

The book is designed to provide practical information, and is particularly aimed at all people involved in designing, specifying and installing signs. It is important that the built environment caters for the needs of everyone, to ensure independent and safe access without undue restriction. Signage forms an important part in creating a barrier-free environment.

There is a considerable amount of published information already available concerning accessible design and, more recently, particularly with the publication of 'Building Sight' in 1995, the design requirements of people with visual impairments have been more readily adopted by design professionals. Access to information, whether in the form of signs or literature, should not be neglected, and the success of RNIB's 'See it Right' campaign has been very encouraging.

The Disability Discrimination Act covers certain types of signage under 'Auxiliary Aids and Services' so that visually impaired people may be given the same access to sign information as everyone else.

Although it has not been the intention to publish an exhaustive book about signage in general, we hope that these recommendations will help people to design and specify an appropriate signage system, to help make buildings and the surrounding environment more accessible to everyone.

The Disability Discrimination Act 1995

With the implementation of the Disability Discrimination Act, inclusive design has been thrown to the forefront of modern environmental design. Design teams, owners and operators are now obliged to recognise the diversity of needs their facilities have to meet, and take reasonable measures to ensure those needs are met.

Part III of the DDA covers the provision of goods, facilities and services, and the selling, letting or management of premises. It means that for those providing services directly to the public it is unlawful to:

- refuse to serve a disabled person for reasons which relate to their disability
- offer a sub-standard service to disabled people
- provide a service on different terms

Service providers include anyone providing a service directly to the general public, whether a public authority, private agency, or an individual and whether for payment or free.

Service providers will be required to make reasonable adjustments to ensure disabled people can use their services easily. This includes the provision of accessible signage, which is an essential element in gaining access to those services.

Reasonable adjustments relate to:

- changes to policies, practices and procedures
- provision of auxiliary aids and services
- making the service accessible by another means
- making the premises more accessible

The first three of these obligations, to make reasonable adjustments, were implemented in October 1999. The fourth requirement, for physical changes to premises, comes into force in 2004 to allow time for suitable adjustments to be made. An indication of the issues that will be taken into account when deciding what is reasonable under the first three obligations to make reasonable adjustments is given in the Code of Practice: 'Rights of Access, Goods, Facilities, Services and Premises' (1999).

A further Code of Practice is due to cover the changes required under the fourth obligation to make premises more accessible by 2004. Legal cases will further define this over time. It may not be sufficient to simply comply with Part M of the Building Regulations, as best practice continues to develop and advance beyond those requirements.

The Act therefore will have a profound significance for all those involved in the management and development of both existing and new buildings, transport facilities and street environments.

Signs would have been likely to count as auxiliary aids and services but the Disability Discrimination (Services and Premises) Regulations state that; 'for the purposes of s21(4) of the DDA, the following are not to be treated as auxiliary aids or services: devices, structures of equipment, installation, operation or maintenance of which would have a permanent effect on the physical fabric of premises, fixtures, fittings, furnishings, furniture, equipment and materials'.

This regulation ceases to have effect when the physical features obligation comes into force in 2004. Therefore, although permanent signage is not covered at present, it will be in future and temporary signs may already be covered.

Ultimately all signage will fall under the Act. It is therefore in the best interests of service providers to ensure that their signage systems follow best practice as outlined in this book. It is also highly recommended that they consult a recognised access consultant for expert advice on access issues when undertaking any new construction or refurbishment works, or to conduct an access audit of their existing premises.

Planned and well thought out signage will mean that people with visual impairments, hearing impairments and those with learning difficulties can function more independently in the external and internal environment. Effective signage will benefit everyone.

Terms of reference

Many people may query the need for a book on signs for people who may not always be able to see them, but it should not be assumed that every person carrying a white cane or using a guide dog is blind. Visual impairment is one of the most common impairments that many people face, and the leaflet, 'Ten things you should know about visual impairment' provides some additional information (see pages 14 and 15).

Figures from 'Disability in Great Britain'* indicate that there are now an estimated 1.97 million people with a significant sight loss. Furthermore, this research also showed that if there was improved assistance 13 per cent of disabled people would go out more, and live more independently, and a further 18 per cent would be encouraged to do so.

If someone has a visual impairment, it means that they may be not only disadvantaged by their sight loss but also by an external environment that does not cater for their needs. Although this book deals with signs and related communication within the built environment and its surroundings, as it affects visually impaired people, the aim is to encourage all those involved in the design, specification and installation of signs to consider the needs of everyone.

The book deals with the concept of 'one sign for all' and covers the design and specification of signs incorporating:

- visual information
- embossed information
- Braille information
- audible information

Some additional wayfinding devices and techniques can be found in the Appendices.

The sign guidelines have been developed through research into best practice, using a cross-section of signs made to specification by several leading sign manufacturers, and tested by a number of user groups. Further information on the testing procedure is contained in the Appendices.

*Disability in Great Britain, DSS, 1999

How to use this book

The book is divided into four main sections.

Section one: Planning – introduces the concept of signage and gives guidance on the assessment of the signage requirements in the environment. It sets out clearly the planning issues that need to be addressed at the outset of a project and will be of use to everyone involved with sign design, specification and installation, as well as to people with little or no experience of sign design.

Section two: Design – considers the technical detail of the design of the message, the incorporation of embossed information and Braille, colour and reading distances. This section will be of particular interest to architects, designers and sign manufacturers.

Section three: Sign practicalities – examines the issues involved in siting signs, including use of lighting, positioning and sign maintenance. It emphasises the importance of maintaining a clean, coherent signage system and will be particularly relevant to those people about to undertake detailed discussion with sign manufacturers.

Section four: The Appendices – provide useful supplementary information and references.

'Ten things you should know about visual impairment'

Extract from RNIB leaflet

1 "Visual defects are one of the most common causes of disability in the world. In Britain nearly one million people are blind or partially sighted – almost one person in sixty. Worldwide, there are over 40 million blind people.

2 The World Health Organisation (WHO) defines 'profound blindness' as the inability to count fingers at a distance of ten feet or less. Partial sight is more difficult to define, but the WHO defines 'severe low vision' as the inability to count fingers at twenty feet or less. (In this book, the term visual impairment is used to include blindness and partial sight).

3 Many different eye defects and diseases can give rise to visual impairment. In Britain the most common are macular degeneration, diabetic retinopathy, glaucoma and cataracts.

4 Different eye conditions create different problems. Very few blind people see nothing at all. A minority can distinguish light but nothing else. Some have no central vision; others have no side vision. Some see everything as a vague blur; others see a patchwork of blanks and defined areas. So some people with impaired vision can see enough to read this leaflet, though they might have difficulty crossing the road.

5 More than 20,000 children are growing up in Britain with a visual impairment. More than half of these youngsters has additional disabilities like deafness, physical disabilities or learning difficulties, which complicate their needs.

6 Four out of five people with impaired vision are over retirement age. Among the over 75s one person in seven is blind or partially sighted. Many of these older people also have other disabilities or illnesses.

7 Eye accidents at home result in 200 hospital visits a day. Most patients recover well but, unfortunately, some lose their sight permanently. Most of these accidents are preventable.

Copies of this leaflet may be obtained from:
Royal National Institute for the Blind
224 Great Portland Street
London W1N 6AA

8 People who register as blind or partially sighted may get special help; some, for instance, can claim disability benefits. But health and social services for people with impaired vision are patchy, and many people receive little or no help from the state. Even if they are entitled to disability benefits, blind people on average have a third less to live on than sighted people.

9 Blind and partially sighted people are just like everyone else, except that they can't see properly. They go to school, college and university; get jobs; bring up families; watch TV; enjoy holidays, friends and hobbies. They may need help to do some or all of these things. For example, blind people may welcome help to find their way around or to cross a busy street but, don't assume that help is needed – always ask first.

10 A little consideration shown by all of us is better than misplaced sympathy. For instance, a parked car on a pavement, or an overhanging hedge, can give a blind person a severe injury at worst, a nasty shock at least".

Types of visual impairment

Sight loss affects different people in different ways although the general effects on the ability to use signage can be grouped into four categories:

Central field loss

People with central field loss cannot see the part of the visual field straight in front of them, although they can still see around the periphery.

The fovea, which is affected when people experience central field loss, is especially important in the perception of fine spatial detail. The fovea is also important in the visual processing that gives a person their perception of three dimensional depth.

Damage to the fovea can create difficulties with perception of fine detail at distance and the perception of depth. Its impairment may also produce problems with fine colour discrimination and create severe difficulties in tasks such as reading.

As a rule, individuals with central field loss retain their general impression of the environment but have great difficulty with the details within it.

Peripheral field loss

People with peripheral field loss can see ahead but lose the periphery of the scene, as if looking through a tube.

Peripheral field loss may affect walking, by creating difficulty in seeing and avoiding obstacles. A person with peripheral field loss may be unaware that someone is approaching them from the side.

However, performance on tests of visual acuity or colour vision may be only slightly reduced in someone with a marked loss of peripheral vision.

Combined central and peripheral field loss

Medical conditions such as diabetes or neurological conditions can result in a combination of central and peripheral field loss depending on the parts of the visual system affected. These individuals will then experience a combination of these difficulties.

Reduced contrast

When contrast perception is reduced the whole visual scene becomes washed out. Light sources give areas a disabling glare which 'white-out' the environment. Cataract is the major cause for general contrast loss.

The images below are representations. Two-dimensional images can only give an impression of a sight condition and will vary according to the individual, the particular stage of the impairment and environmental factors, such as varying light conditions.

Central field loss

Peripheral field loss

Combined central and peripheral field loss

Reduced contrast

1

Planning

1.1

What is a sign?

A sign is a means of conveying information about direction, location, safety or a form of action. Signs are most important to people who are unfamiliar with their surroundings or who need to know how to do something, such as find the fire exit or operate a door entry system. Sign readers may be anxious, confused, lost or nervous and a proportion will have a visual impairment that makes location and understanding of a sign more difficult than usual.

A successful sign system should minimise such anxiety and confusion. It should be easy to understand and people with a visual impairment should not be placed at a disadvantage. Signs should be:

- clear
- concise
- consistent

When considering a new sign system it is essential to spend time at the planning stage. Rigorous examination of the building or wider site, the functions it houses and their implications for signage will pay dividends as it maximises the likelihood of achieving the optimum solution and minimises the possibility of making expensive mistakes.

1.2

The four sign groups

Most signs can be divided into four functional groups:

Information signs
These are the main signs for orientation; they would include the building, car park and other internal signs identifying main locations inside the building and including directories, maps and plans, covering the whole site, externally and internally.

Direction signs
These direct users to destinations using arrows and can include directional text. Often they carry several destinations in a bank of signs and care has to be taken with the use of arrows to avoid confusion.

In pedestrian environments finger post signs are often specified, but their height, combined with the small size of the message on the finger, makes them very hard to read. The use of finger posts should be avoided.

Identification (or location) signs
These signs – always without an arrow – are installed at individual destinations to indicate the location of a facility or a service, a room or a person, once a destination has been reached. Some location signs can be short; others may contain several levels of information.

Safety, fire safety and mandatory signs
These signs are essential for the safety of users and can be either warning or prohibition signs. They will be positioned at strategic points to give warning of a hazard. They include exit signs, fire exit signs, fire safety signs and details about fire equipment. This category also includes mandatory signs which are usually characterised by a special colour and shape, ie. white letters on a blue square.

Information signs
are used to identify sites, buildings or spaces and are also used on Directories

Direction signs
usually have arrows attached to them

Identification (or location) signs
are used for numbering or naming rooms

Safety, fire safety and mandatory signs
are covered by BSI Standards and should be taken from these Standards

1.3

The initial appraisal of the site or building

Signs are only one of several tools available to people finding their way around a site. They may also refer to:

- colour labelling of floors or departments
- architectural features unique to certain areas
- the views from the windows
- plans

People with a visual impairment will also pay particular attention to:

- sound quality determined by floor finishes such as muffled sounds in carpeted areas and echoing sounds on hardwood floors

- changes in floor construction, for example: solid to suspended sounds on hardwood floors

- tactile surface underfoot

- colour contrast at the junction of walls and floors, walls and doors, floors and furniture and other critical surfaces

A good signage scheme will work in conjunction with the orientation clues provided by the site to make clear the identification of, and the direction to, certain key destinations. These could include:

1 approach
2 entrance / exit
3 main lobby or reception
4 communal facilities such as cafeteria, library, toilets
5 departments and offices
6 fire exits
7 parking and garages
8 public transport drop-off points etc

When making the initial appraisal of a site, it is important to record the information in a manageable way. Plans of each floor are very useful as they allow the appraiser to mark the forms of destination as listed on the previous page, together with the routes a building user might take to reach them. Remember that visitors may not proceed directly to one destination and then out again; they may break their journey with a visit to a toilet or need to go to several destinations. In both cases signs should enable people to continue their journey through a site or building without the need to retrace their steps to locate an appropriate sign.

As routes intersect and diverge, the user will be confronted with the need to make a decision. Signs are essential at these points. If the route to a destination is long, albeit continuous, confirmation signs along the route at reasonable and appropriate intervals are helpful because they reassure visitors that they are going the right way.

Once plans are marked with approximate locations for information signs, direction signs and identification (or location signs), they should be reviewed once more for fire safety.

The location of routes leading to exits, fire fighting equipment and refuges, will usually dictate which safety signs are used and their location.

1.4

Range of action

The first assessment of sign and content

Having decided upon an appropriate level of action, it is now possible to develop the material collected in the initial appraisal of the building (see section1.3). Whereas that was primarily a desk study, this assessment relies upon a close inspection of the site for greater accuracy.

For example, the initial appraisal may have highlighted the need for a sign on the first floor landing directing building users to the lifts, the toilets and the library. The site visit will enable the person responsible for signs to decide whereabouts on the landing the sign could best be positioned. Detailed positioning is not required at this stage, but an indication only, such as 'on the landing wall, to the left of the lifts'.

In this example, signs on landings above Floor One that carry similar information should be placed in the same relative location. Consistency is very important as it reduces the amount of work needed to make sense of a building.

The sign content can be kept fairly vague at this point. It is enough to know what information each sign should contain; how it should say it is covered in section 2.1.

The site visit will also uncover where plans and directories should be located. They could be in a reception or lobby area, and on each floor close to the stairs, lifts or escalators. Both plans and directories are very useful as they provide an opportunity for the visitor to pause and absorb information about the building. They should be placed where they do not interfere with the flow of human traffic.

Safety signs, including all prohibition, mandatory, warning, safety signs and fire safety signs, are all covered by legislation and design guidelines are issued by the BSI Standards. Reference should be made to the relevant British Standards for information on sign shape, message and colour. Logical and consistent positioning of all safety signs is essential for their accessibility to people with sight impairments.

Some basic guidelines on sign location

1 Think carefully about possible obstructions of signs. It is no good choosing a location for a sign in a reception area if it will be regularly obscured by deliveries, for example. Remember that external signs may become partially covered by plants or trees in leaf, during the summer.

2 Consider whether the sign itself may become an obstruction. Suspended and wall mounted signs should be located at an adequate height to avoid obstruction, but care must be taken not to place them too far above a person's sightline. Placing signs in the middle of a route on the basis that they will be more easily noticed will cause problems for people with sight impairments. A floor mounted sign will cause an obvious hazard. A suspended sign placed in the middle of a route may cause difficulty in locating or reading the sign due to a changing or inconsistent background.

3 Consider whether a sign will be read from a distance (such as across a car park or at the end of a corridor) or close-up. This will have a bearing on text height and consequently on sign size (see section 2.4).

4 Remember that locations for signs require good illumination; avoid areas that are gloomy and cannot receive supplementary lighting. Section 3.1 considers illumination and glare in detail.

5 Room identification signs should ideally be located at eye level, on the wall immediately adjacent to the latch side of the door. Where a sign cannot be placed on the wall, for example, where there is no available space, the sign can be placed on the door. Ensure that all room identification signs are positioned at the same height throughout the building, ideally within the 1400 - 1700mm band (see section 3.2).

Some basic guidelines on sign content

1 Information can be better understood if it is grouped together either alphabetically, or by floor, or by department.

2 Too many messages on a sign should be avoided. A hierarchical system may be used, with a further breakdown of information provided as people progress along a route to a destination. Several small groups of messages are easier to read than one large list (see diagram opposite).

3 Room identification signs should be simple and concise. Once a name has been chosen, it should be used consistently throughout the building.

4 Abbreviations should be avoided because they can be particularly confusing for people with a visual impairment.

5 Descriptive words such as 'Personnel' or 'Accounts' do not need to be qualified by the use of 'Department' or 'Division'.

6 Visually impaired people can recognise numbers more easily than names, and numbers can, of course, be larger than text without occupying as much space.

Wherever appropriate, signage should incorporate information which includes the following elements:

- visual
- embossed and Braille (see section 2.3)
- audible (see section 2.7)

When a decision has been made about the hierarchy of information to adopt within a building, it should be applied consistently to avoid confusion.

When the first assessment of sign content and location has been completed, a considerable amount of information will have been amassed. Plans of the building will form an important part of this as they provide the key to the understanding of the rough schedule containing the sign details. The next stage is to consider the sign messages in detail (section 1) and the design of the sign itself (section 2). Ultimately, a formal schedule can be drawn up for discussion with a sign supplier (see section 3.3).

Avoid long lists of names on Directories

Cafeteria
Cashier
First Aid
Lifts
Maintenance
Parking
Security
Telephones
Toilets

Shorter columns are easier to read and remember

Cafeteria	Lifts	Security
Cashier	Maintenance	Telephones
First Aid	Parking	Toilets

Plan of entrance lobby. The Directory should be in a prominent position opposite the entrance

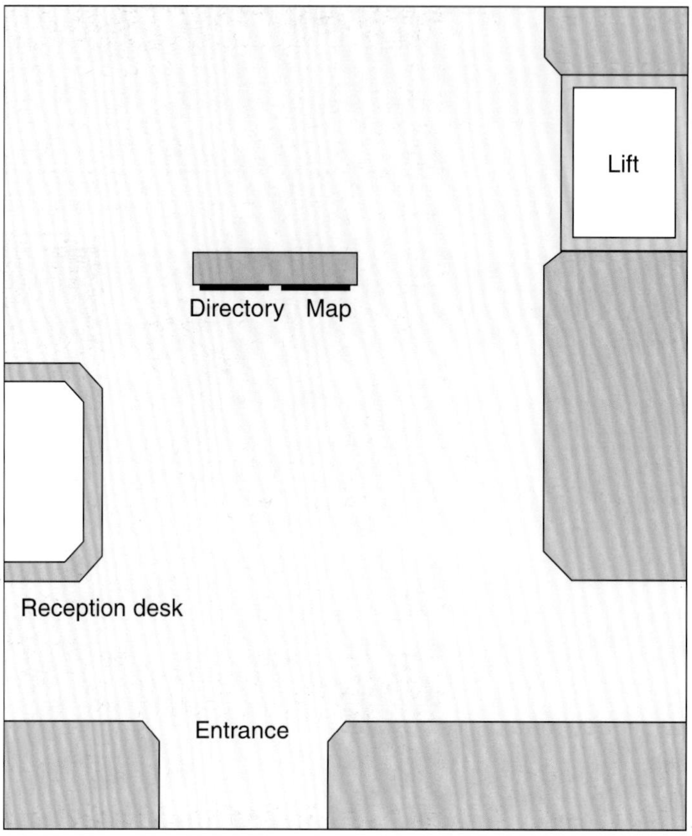

Consistent positions for direction signs on landings are essential

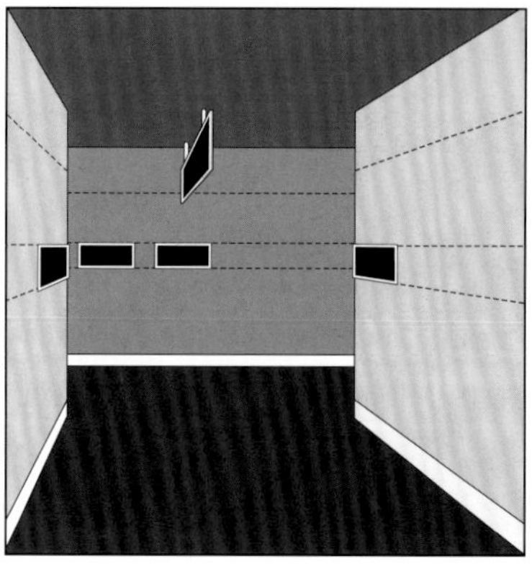

Plan diagrams of direction signs at corridor intersections

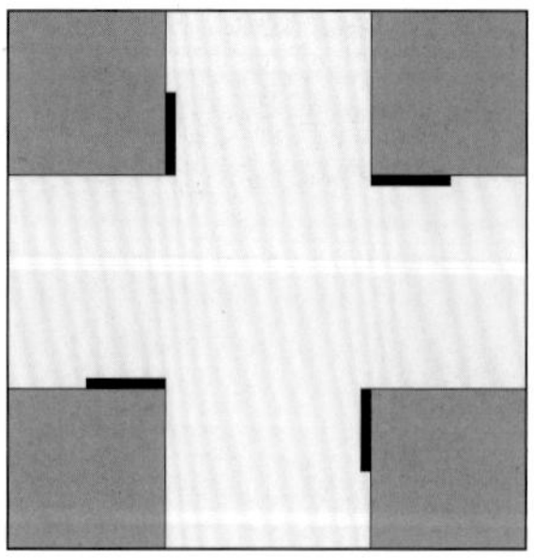

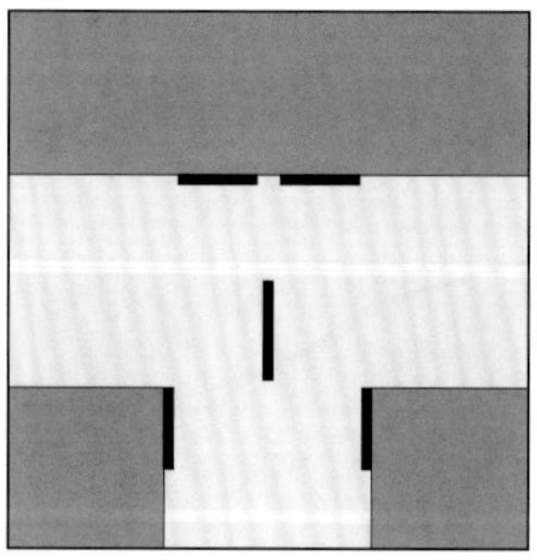

Consistency of sign position is important

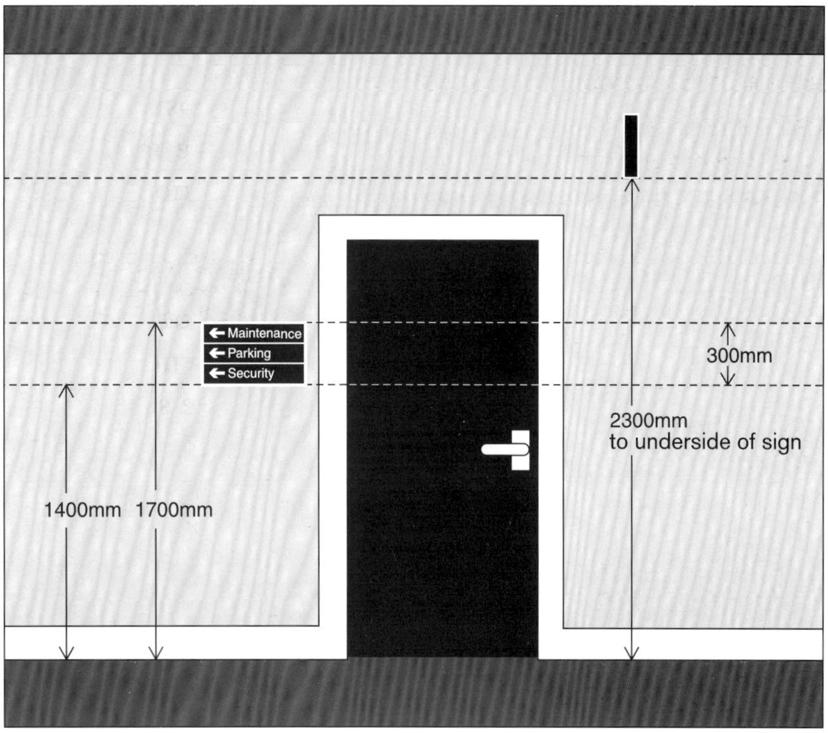

Signs should be at the same height throughout the building except for signs which include a control element eg. lifts or door entry systems

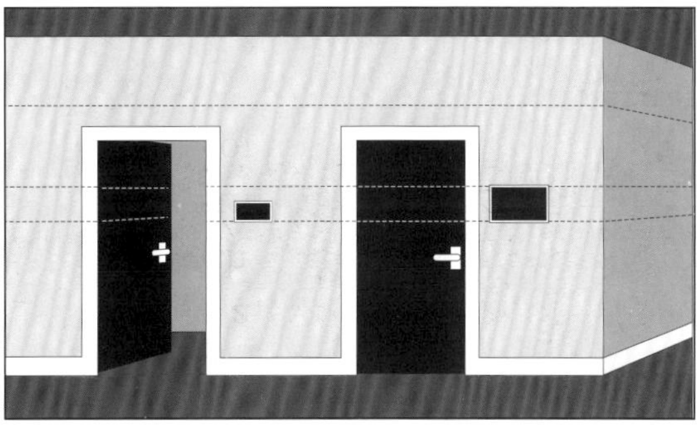

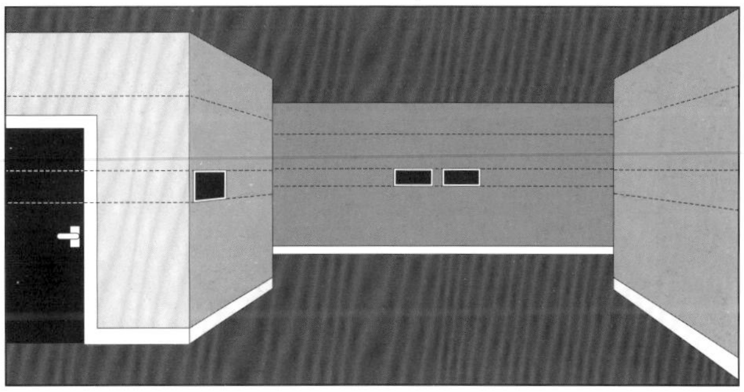

2

Design

2.1

Language, wording and punctuation

Language is one of the most important factors in sign design; people need very clear, unambiguous messages in simple, understandable formats.

Clarity

The language should utilise words which the user understands and should relate to the user's needs. If messages are technical or complicated in their wording, many people will be discouraged and will need to seek assurance from others. Official terms which may be unfamiliar should be avoided.

Consistency

Terminology should be consistent; ie. the words used on a directory at the entrance should be identical to those found on a specific department door.

Conciseness

It is important to remember when planning signs to keep information to a minimum; only give enough information at any point to enable the user to accomplish their current objective. Too much information confuses everyone and will either be ignored or forgotten.

This is especially important when designing information signs but care should be taken to ensure that brevity does not compromise meaning. Identification (or location) signs are inherently simple because they usually carry only one destination name.

Where possible messages should be short enough to be read in passing, although plans and directories will require a longer pause. Floor plans are a useful complement to directories as they can carry the detail while the directory lists each floor's main destinations.

Although wording and punctuation are open to subjective interpretation, there are some guidelines that are positively helpful to everyone.

Capital letters

Improved legibility will be achieved if the first word of each of the key words begins with a capital letter; subsequent words should begin with a lower case letter:

Accounts
Reception and General Enquiries

Names for specific job titles, places or people should have capital letters at the beginning of each word:

Finance Director
Head of Personnel
Manager, Research Unit

Exceptions to this guideline are traditional, customary or specific words required by legislation and written in capital letters, eg. EXIT or TAXI.

Titles and initials

Titles and initials are usually more legible if full stops are omitted between initials. Titles, first names and surnames are more easily read beginning with a capital letter and continuing in lower case:

Dr J C Thompson
Ms K S Powell

Punctuation

For clarity, it is better to use punctuation sparingly and avoid the use of full stops at the end of messages.

Two destinations are easier to read if placed on two separate lines

Car Park
Pedestrian Entrance

Car Park, Pedestrian Entrance

Abbreviations

Avoid abbreviations because they can be misinterpreted.

Other means of identification

Sometimes words are not needed for identification, for example, where there is a group of signs relating to a large department, it may be preferable to group them by colour, eg:

- all engineering departments – marine blue
- all electronic departments – orange
- administration – brown

Care should be taken when adding colours to a sign system because this will add another level of required understanding which will have to be explained, ie. that engineering is blue and electronics is orange.

It is also preferable to avoid using colours that have a safety meaning, eg. green which is used for fire exits (see BS 5378 and BS 5499). Certain shades of red, yellow and blue are also safety colours. (See section 2.6 for guidance on the choice of colours that will produce sufficient contrast to highlight messages to assist visually impaired users).

Symbols

In addition to words, some signs, particularly directional signs, are often supplemented by specific pictorial devices such as arrows and/or symbols. Well recognised symbols are often better than words for most types of vision, but they are particularly useful for visually impaired people because they can be larger than the equivalent text message. In addition, many symbols are internationally recognised, overcoming the language barrier; public information, road traffic, safety and fire safety are among these.

The success of symbols depends on simplicity, legibility and a good recognition factor, the objective being that the symbol should be immediately recognisable. Four of the most easily recognised ones are shown on this page.

In addition, there are several internationally recognised symbols relating to people with disabilities which should be used wherever they are appropriate:

- accessibility for disabled people
- symbol for visual disability
- hearing impairment
- text telephone (TDD symbol)

Standard versions are covered in BSI and ISO publications and should always be used in preference to any others (see Appendices).

Where dual language signs are mandatory or advisable, serious consideration should be given to using symbols as well.

Symbols can be a useful quick recognition device for visually impaired people who may then read the accompanying tactile or Braille message. Embossed symbols can be particularly useful (see section 2.3).

Arrows

Arrows are one of the most useful symbols in any signing system. Although everyone believes that they can design an arrow, they are misused more than any other graphic form.

Correct ISO arrow

It is advisable always to use the ISO (International Standards Organisation) 7001 recommendation, an arrow whose ends are parallel with the main stem, not cut off at 90 degrees (see example left).

Avoid!

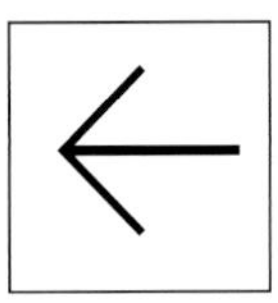

Avoid:

1 Arrows which have the same dimensions all round. They look top-heavy and lack direction.

2 Arrows which look like chicken foot imprints because their message can be ambiguous.

3 Arrows with double angles.

4 Mass use of arrows

Arranging arrows on signs

On large board signs where a number of messages are listed, eg. at entrances to buildings, a group of messages should be preceded by a single arrow, rather than using individual arrows for each message.

On combination signs, where several arrows are required in close proximity, they are more intelligible if they are arranged according to direction:

- left up
- left
- left down and straight ahead
- right up
- right
- right down and straight ahead

It is also important that arrows are arranged so that arrow location corresponds to direction and to avoid too great a scanning distance between the end of a line of text and the directional arrow (see diagrams on pages 39 and 40).

Arrows and their directions

Messages on signs should be aligned to the right or to the left according to the direction indicated by the arrow. For example:

- arrows indicating direction to the left, straight ahead or down should be placed on the left-hand side of the first message
- arrows indicating direction to the right should be placed on the right-hand side of the message. In this case, it would be helpful to use a locator on the left hand margin

Care should be taken to avoid giving misleading directional information, eg. showing a fire exit sign with arrows pointing left *and* right. People leaving the building in a hurry may be unable to choose which direction to take.

Arrows pointing left precede the message

Several messages

When a sign carries several messages of equal emphasis – and the direction indicated is the same – only one arrow, in front of the message, is necessary.

Where one message is subsidiary to another, and it is in a smaller size of lettering, an arrow should only be included with the main message.

Placement of arrows

When positioning arrows of a 45 degree indication, care must be taken in their use because they have no inherent exactness and can be open to misinterpretation. In general they should be reserved for stairs, escalators, ramps and diagonal routes across open areas only.

If in doubt, it may be better to disregard any change in floor level and use a 90 degree arrow to the left or a 90 degree arrow to the right.

Arrows pointing right follow the message

Direction to the left - arrow is on the left of the message

Direction to the right - arrow is on the right of the message

Incorrect:
too great a scanning distance between the message and the arrow

Incorrect:
text and arrow should be ranged right

2.2

Letterform selection

Letterforms or typefaces for signs should be legible and easy to obtain; AppleMac or PC typefaces are usually available through any designer or sign manufacturer and can be previewed in any typeface catalogue.

One of the most universally used typefaces for signs is Helvetica Medium which has been used by many hospitals and other institutions. Although commendable for its legibility, there are many other sans serif faces which are equally good, and which have more character, for example: Akzidenz Grotesque, Arial, Avant Garde, Futura.

Some seriffed typefaces, if their serifs are not too large, also have good legibility and are often more suitable for use where a different character is required. For example, the following have proven track records: Baskerville, Bembo, Century Schoolbook, Sabon, Times New Roman.

The choice of letterform will depend on the building, or site, and its historic context. The best effect will be achieved by the appropriate choice of letterform, colour and materials.

Serifed typefaces are not suitable for embossed signs which should always be reproduced in a simple sans serif such as Helvetica.

A selection of sans serif typefaces. The letter O should be almost round and the letter thickness should be consistent; neither too heavy nor too thin

Akzidenz Grotesque	**123456789**
Arial	123456789
Avant Garde	123456789
Futura	**123456789**
Helvetica	**123456789**

Some of the most legible serifed typefaces. Look at the numerals too, to see if they are clear and consistent

Baskerville	123456789
Bembo	123456789
Century Schoolbook	**123456789**
Sabon	123456789
Times New Roman	123456789

Things to avoid:

- exaggerated typefaces that are either too expanded or too condensed, too decorative or too fanciful, because they will detract from the readability of the sign
- italics or scripts because they are often illegible
- typefaces with over-long ascenders or descenders because they may present legibility problems
- very bold letterforms where the white space inside letters disappears – although occasional use can sometimes be helpful in breaking-up long pieces of information
- too many type sizes on any one sign
- when selecting the range of sizes to use, consideration should be given to the relationship between distance and legibility. (see section 2.4).

✗ Old English is exaggerated

✗ *Italics are not very clear*

✗ **This face is too condensed**

✗ *Scripts like this are illegible*

2.3

Sizes for letters, symbols, Braille and embossed characters

The minimum sizes for text and embossed characters, symbols and Braille information depend upon location of the sign and the reading distance. To assist users with visual impairments, the characters should be larger than has until now been the convention, but it should be acknowledged that some people would not be able to distinguish the message however large the characters. It is important that character size is related to reading distance because too large a character at close reading distance may not be legible either. An embossed character height of less than 15mm (capital height) starts to become difficult to read from touch alone.

Long distance reading
For example, at building entrances or for house numbers, a minimum character size of 150mm is recommended.

Medium range reading
For example, for identification signs in reception areas or direction signs in corridors, a character size of 50-100mm is recommended.

Close-up reading
For example, on directories or wall mounted information signs, a minimum character size of 15-25mm is recommended.

Information hierarchy
Where character size is intended to inform the building user of hierarchy, for example, in functions or departments, the minimum character size appropriate for the reading distance should be used for the least important information.

Symbols
Where space permits, symbols should be at least 100mm in height overall.

Embossed signs
Embossed signs are essential for people with no sight, or whose vision is only sufficient to locate a sign but not to distinguish individual characters. Because embossed signs take longer to read by touch, it is even

more important that the messages should be concise, unambiguous and brief.

Embossed signs are, by their nature, always read close-up and should be positioned where they can be easily touched. The ideal range of heights for positioning should be between 1400mm and 1700mm above finished floor level.

Signs should be embossed not engraved. The characters should be raised from the surrounding surface by 1mm-1.5mm, and the thickness of each stroke of the letter should be such that both sides of the stroke can be felt with the finger in one pass. The minimum character height will vary between 15mm and 50mm depending on the space available and the reading distance required. The stroke width should be between 1.5mm and 2mm for a 15mm letter height and pro rata for larger letters.

Inter-character spacing should be increased between 20-30 per cent, depending on the selected font; the inter-word spacing should be increased by approximately 25 per cent. Characters should not have sharp edges but should be clearly defined with rounded or chamfered edges.

A sans serif typeface should be specified.

Depth of embossing for text is 1-1.5mm

Reading an embossed sign in the vertical plane is not comfortable so, if the face of the sign can be inclined at 45-60 degrees from the horizontal, it provides a more natural position for the hand.

Braille information

In the UK, around 19,000 people use Braille regularly. Braille is a system of raised dots, which enables visually impaired people to read with their fingers. It is made up of patterns of six dots, allowing 63 possible combinations, which correspond to letters of the alphabet, numbers, punctuation and letter groups or words.

Basic system

Words are formed by the use of all the possible combinations of six dots, numbered and arranged as shown on page 48.

Numbers and punctuation

The first ten letters preceded by the number sign (dots 3,4,5,6) represent numbers. Combinations of dots in the lower part of the cell form punctuation marks.

Grade 1 Braille

Grade 1 Braille is letter-for-letter transcription which can be read by all Braille users, and it is the first stage of learning to read Braille but, because it is bulky, it is usually replaced by Grade 2 Braille which is a contracted form.

As a general rule, Grade 1 Braille should be used for single words and short descriptions, eg. 'Push bar to open'. Grade 2 Braille should be used for longer descriptions and sentences.

Grade 2 Braille

Grade 2 Braille consists of contractions added to the combinations to represent common letter groups such as 'the' and 'for'; the contractions are too numerous to list here. Grade 2 may be appropriate for longer instructions, ie. an opening plaque or site description.

Braille 2 is also widely used for the production of books, magazines and leaflets. It occupies less space than Grade 1 but all Braille is bulky. For example, using Braille, one A4 printed page would need approximately two and a half pages.

Dimensions for English Standard Braille

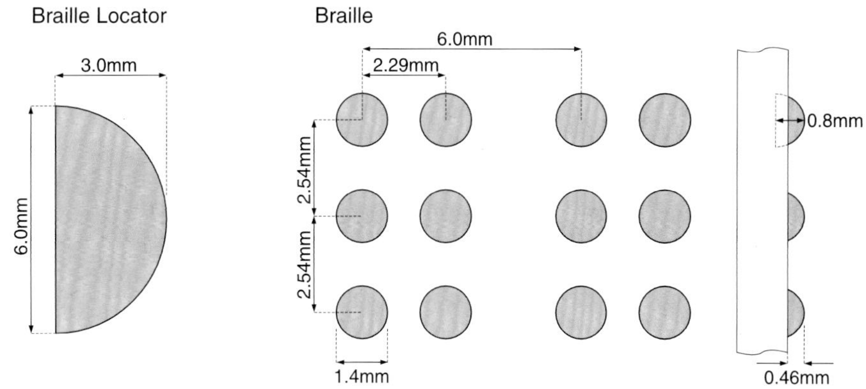

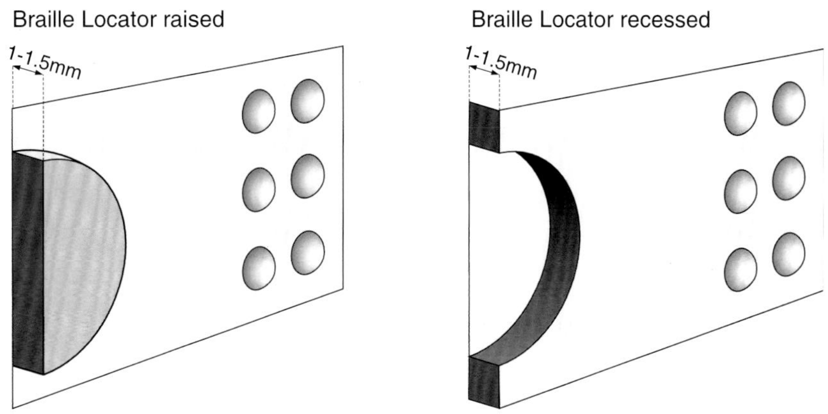

Practical considerations

1 Braille can be incorporated into signboards and should be located directly below the text (and arrow) and ranged left. A small embossed arrow can be used to indicate direction, either before or after the Braille.

2 A locator along the left-hand edge of the signboard should be provided. This allows people to determine the exact location of the Braille, by sliding a finger down until they reach an indented notch, or similar mark, to indicate the Braille location.

3 Because Braille is felt by the pads of the fingers not the finger tips, it is important that no obstructions, such as frames or raised borders, should surround it.

4 The Braille to be used should be English Standard Braille (see Braille specification on next page).

5 Braille dots should be rounded.

6 Braille does not differentiate between upper and lower characters.

Grade 1 Braille

The illustration shows Grade 1 Braille as black dots, actual Braille would be embossed

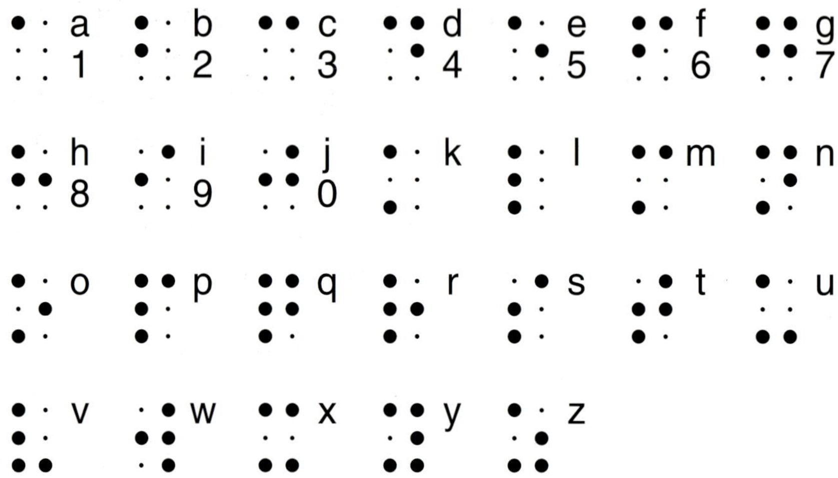

When symbols are used, Braille should always be positioned under the message

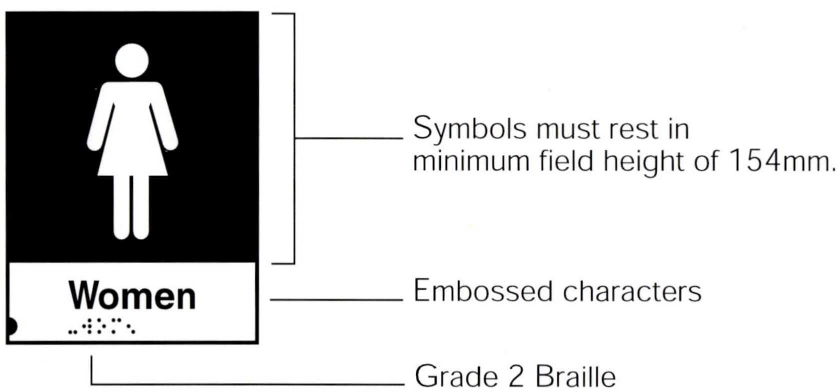

For panels with symbols on them, eg. toilets, it is acceptable to centre the text on the panel and to position the Braille, ranged left, below the text.

Fire safety signs

Fire safety signs are mandatory and must comply with the requirements of Health & Safety (Safety Signs and Signals) Regulations and BS 5499. These signs should be positioned close to relevant fire appliances, alarms or fire points and be applied consistently throughout the building.

Although the relevant Standards do not cover embossed information, it can easily be incorporated into standard safety signs to comply with legislative requirements.

2.4

Reading distance and letter size

Section 2.3 gives an indication of the minimum character sizes for close-up, medium and long distance viewing. This section develops the data to enable the selection of optimum size for maximum legibility.

The graph on the next page shows the relationship between character size and reading distance for people with 6/9 visual acuity (approximated to the UK standard for driving), 6/60 vision (below this line, someone registered as partially sighted would probably not be able to read this text) and 3/60 vision (below this line, someone registered as blind would probably not be able to read this text).

Height versus distance chart

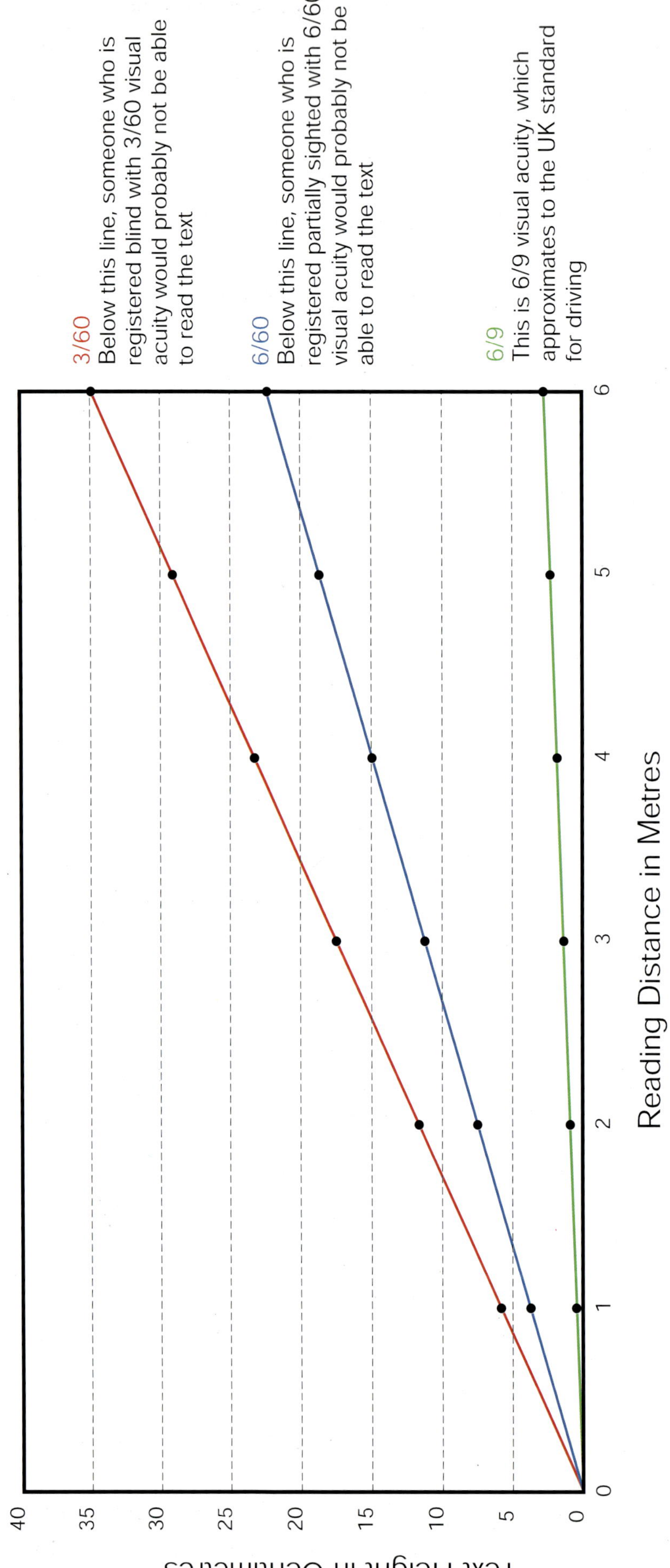

2.5

Layout, space, capitals and lower case

The importance of space

Because legibility depends as much on the use of space as the selection of letterform, it is important to consider the types of spacing which assist legibility. There are three:

- space between letters
- space between words
- space between lines

For visually impaired people, it is desirable to increase the space between letters, words and lines between 20 and 30 per cent, depending on the selected letterform.

Line spacing

Consistent line spacing is also essential, not only for legibility but for the alignment of messages which may be positioned next to each other. In general, people with visual impairments need a 15-20 per cent increase in line spacing.

Effective layout

The layout of a sign – the way that the messages are arranged – like space, is as important as the letterforms selected for it.

Text ranging

One of the most important ways of controlling layout is through the alignment of text. There are three basic alignments:

1. ranging left
(aligning on the left-hand side, ragged on the right)
2. ranging right
(aligning on the right-hand side, ragged on the left)
3. centred
(aligning on a centre point)

For direction signs, the text should be ranged according to the direction of the arrow. Left and straight ahead signs should be ranged left, right direction signs should be ranged right (see section 2.1).

Margins

Margins are sometimes helpful because they allow more tonal contrast between the message and the background.

Borders

A border is also sometimes useful to ensure an effective colour contrast, but the width of the border should not overpower the letters; 10 per cent of the lower case letter height is a good guide.

Legibility

Words are more legible and easier to remember if lower case letters are used. Even with blurred vision, words with capital and lower case letters are easier to identify because they make unique shapes.

Readability

Too many words on a sign, or too many messages on a bank of signs, make readability and retention of messages difficult.

Wrong spacing. Ascenders and descenders merge together ✗

> The spacing between lines is critical for readability. For example, the spacing between these lines is too close. It makes ascenders and descenders merge together.

Normal line spacing. Usually too small for visually impaired people ✗

> The spacing between lines is critical for readability. This is normal spacing between lines of text for people without a sight impairment.

Wide inter-line spacing. Essential for clear legibility

> The spacing between lines is critical for readability. Visually impaired people need more space between lines of text to help legibility.

Ranged left text is the
easiest to read

Avoid ranged right text,
if possible

Avoid centralised text,
if possible

How many words per line?

Using too many letters or words on a line can cause visual clutter. A suggested maximum for legibility would be 12-14 letters per line, including spaces, or 2 to 3 words per line, depending on the typeface and the space between the lines. Conciseness is important, particularly where people may be reading by touch.

Capitals and lower case

Although capital letters were the norm for most signs up to the 1960s, the necessity for recognition of signs at greater speeds on motorways led to research into the use of lower case letters and symbols (The Anderson Committee 1962).

Legibility tests for motorways, airports, hospitals and other major complexes suggest that people reading words and phrases from a distance recognise them as much for their shape as for their content.

Lower case letters, because of their ascenders and descenders, make distinctive and memorable images. Research conducted by Carol Tan in the USA* (Tan 1991) compared an established road signing typeface (US Standard Highway Alphabet series D and E(m) with lowercase) with Helvetica, VAG Rounded, Dot Matrix and Serif Gothic. The results of the research showed that for the typefaces used in the study the sans serif typefaces are more legible than serif typefaces.

Signs showing more than five messages create confusion and may be ignored. The exception is on a directory where several shorter messages can be absorbed.

From tests with both sighted and visually impaired people, signs which use a mixture of both capitals and lower case letters are the most satisfactory solution for most types of vision.

*'Alternative Highway Sign Alphabet for Older Drivers"
Texas A&M University, College Station, TX
Carol Tan, 1991

Braille and embossed signs

There is some debate about whether lower case letters are helpful for embossed signs – the letters a,e,g and i can cause confusion in some letterforms (see Appendices – testing procedures). However JMU recommends that the same combination of upper and lower case letters are used so as to give consistency between visual and embossed sign formats.

Words are more legible and easier to remember if lower case letters are used because they make word shapes

RECEPTION
Reception

RECEPTION
Reception

Even with blurred vision, upper and lower case words are more memorable

2.6

Colour and contrast

Basic principle

The efficiency of any signage system relies heavily on the ability of the user to detect, recognise and read the sign. Therefore contrast, which may be described as the difference in colour – or difference in light reflection – between all the elements of the sign is essential, eg.

- between the background (bricks, trees etc) and the signboard, and
- between the signboard and the text or symbol on it

Some people have low colour vision which affects their perception of some colours; for example, people who have visual impairments often have a reduction in their ability to recognise some reds, greens and blues. They may also have a reduction in recognition between two similar colours such as blue and green but, although colour differentiation may be affected, they may still be able to detect tonal differences. Tonal differences are far more effective than differences in hue (ie red, green, blue).

Colour selection

Colour selection is also important in creating the desired atmosphere and ambience in an interior; although signs need to be recognised, they should also complement the interior design.

Rooms and spaces that are finished in shiny, patterned or busy surfaces may create visual confusion and discomfort which, in turn, will affect navigation and wayfinding. Choosing a bright, saturated colour for a sign background is not always the best solution.

Buildings with more than three storeys, with similar floor layouts on each level, may present problems in identification of each level. Some sign systems use a different colour for each level, but the success of this system relies upon the user's ability to identify and recognise the difference between the colours. Using too many colours, or colours which are too similar in hue and tone (eg. orange and red) should not be used for this purpose. Some of the most successful signing systems use white with one or two additional colours;

for example motorway signs, road warning signs and original British Airports signs. If in doubt, use as few colours as possible and avoid colours which may conflict with fire and safety signs (see Appendices).

Maintenance should also be considered when specifying colours. Using several colours may increase repair and maintenance costs; it may be better to invest in embossed and Braille equivalents instead.

Some colours fade or are 'fugitive' in bright sunlight; these include purples, bright oranges, some reds and greens. Although paint specifications increasingly improve, using 'fugitive' colours may cause maintenance problems later.

Black and white can cause glare but reversed letters, white on a dark ground, always look bigger

Colour combinations

As already outlined, the contrast between letters or symbols and their background is as important as size for everyone when reading signs.

Black and white provide the most obvious contrast but can cause halation for some people due to the extreme contrast and glare. Although not always appropriate to the building or site, JMU advises that white lettering on a dark signboard (not necessarily black) gives good legibility if accompanied by a matt surface.

In determining colour combinations, it is important to check the background against which the sign is to be seen. For example, black letters on a white sign would not be helpful if positioned on a white wall.

External colour contrasts

The chart reproduced on the next page has been produced by JMU to give guidance on the colour contrast which should be used against some of the most commonly used backgrounds for signboards such as brick, stone, whitewashed walls or green vegetation.

Contrast derives from the light reflectance factor of the colours used, not the difference between the colours, eg. light green against dark green.

External colour contrasts

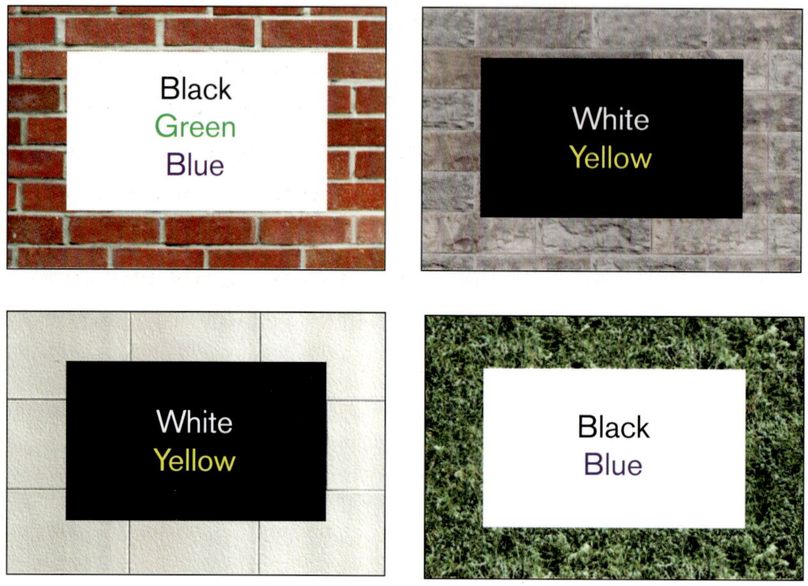

Background	*Signboard*	*Legend*
Red brick or dark stone	White	Black / blue / green
Light brick or light stone	Black / dark	White / yellow
Whitewashed wall	Black / dark	White / yellow
Green vegetation	White	Black / blue / green

Sometimes a border between background and signboard is useful

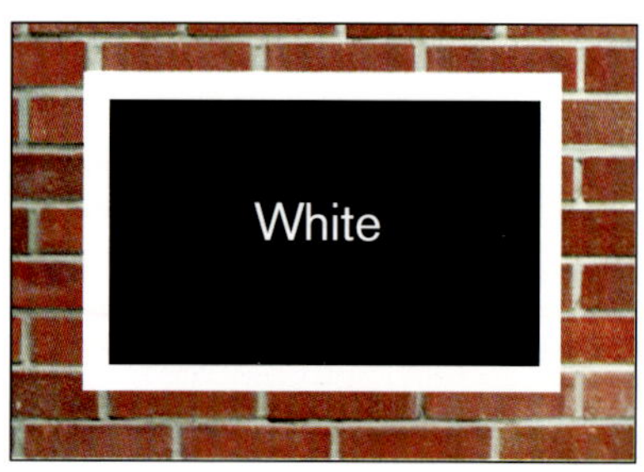

Ideally the contrast between wall and sign panel should be 70 per cent; the gloss factor should be 50 per cent which will give adequate legibility but still facilitate cleaning.

Identifiable colours

If signs are required for a large complex which includes many functions or departments, it is worth remembering that for normal recognition, there are twelve colours*, listed below, that can be easily recognised and named without resorting to qualifying descriptions. Only one shade of each colour is included to avoid terminology problems between two shades of the same colour, ie. sage green/grass green, or colours being described as 'pale' or 'dark'.

For accurate colour specification, the reference number of the colour should always be quoted and obtained from a reputable paint manufacturer, based on recognised colour specification standards eg. Pantone, RAL, NCS, British Standards etc.

*By kind permission of 'Orientation and Wayfinding in Public Buildings'. Public Works, Canada, 1988

Red	Orange	Pink	Grey
Yellow	Green	Brown	White
Blue	Purple	Black	Beige

Please note that using these colours in combinations will not necessarily produce the right results in terms of contrast and legibility.

2.7

Audible signs

Electronic wayfinding systems herald a new era of independence for blind and partially sighted people.

These products, which give a spoken message to the user when they visit establishments, greatly improve accessibility to the range of facilities.

Wayfinding systems commercially available are:

- Infra-red systems (IR)
- Radio Frequency systems (RF)
- Passive Infra-red (PIR) and manually operated systems

Infra-red signs

Infra-red signs give a personal spoken message to help blind and partially sighted people to find their way.

They can be used to give the information that is available on the visual signs. Placed at junctions, infra-red signs give information on what is ahead and to the left or right. The user automatically picks up the messages through a personal receiver.

The message is heard personally by the user, through an earpiece or small speaker attached to the lapel, and will not interfere with other people or devices. The system uses an infra-red beam; when the user enters the beam the receiver speaks the message.

Radio Frequency signs

A Radio Frequency sign is a sign device that produces an audible message through a loudspeaker to help blind and partially sighted people find their way.

Radio Frequency signs only function when a user carrying a user's activator card walks past. The system is used to give information (like visual signs or architectural features) that blind or partially sighted people would miss.

The system can also be used to operate devices as well as give messages. For example, it can be used to open an electric door, raise a barrier or operate a remote bell or buzzer.

The system works using audible location. When the user walks within range of the sign, a radio signal emitted by the sign is reflected by the user's activator card to make the sign speak the message.

PIR activated speaking sign

This sign can be used to warn, inform or alert a person to a situation by speaking a pre-recorded message. This message is then activated by a Passive Infra-red Detector (PIR) that detects body heat, eg. when someone passes the sign. A high quality audio message can be recorded on to the unit using an in-built microphone. The recording will remain in memory even when the power source is removed.

The speaking sign can be used in many applications such as welcoming people at the entrance to a building, warning of obstacles, alerting people to dangers etc.

Manually operated signs

These audio-visual signs consist of an illuminated or non-illuminated poster case and digital sound recorder. When the button is pressed on the display, the audio message is played. The messages can be 20 or 60 seconds long.

2.8

Lifts

Lifts

Lifts are an important circulation aid to people with disabilities. They open up otherwise inaccessible areas to wheelchair users and provide an alternative to stairs and the hazards these pose to people with sight impairments. They do need, however, to be carefully designed and detailed:

- the lift itself should be highly visible and differentiated in treatment from doors to rooms
- the lift buttons in the lobby should be placed on the wall adjacent to the lift door rather than on the door frame
- colours and tones should be chosen to give clear contrast between controls and their background
- an embossed indication should also be provided
- the lift button in the lobby should be easily seen against the background
- an embossed indication should also be provided
- control button panels and floor indicators should be mounted in the range of 900-1200mm above finished floor level (both inside and outside the lift)
- the floor number should be repeated on the wall opposite the lift door, if possible
- horizontally arranged controls outside the lift are a useful alternative to the conventional vertically arranged controls, especially for wheelchair users.

The lift diagrams on the following two pages show the recommended dimensions and demonstrate the importance of colour contrast between surfaces such as doors, frames, floor numbers and buttons etc.

Lift – front view

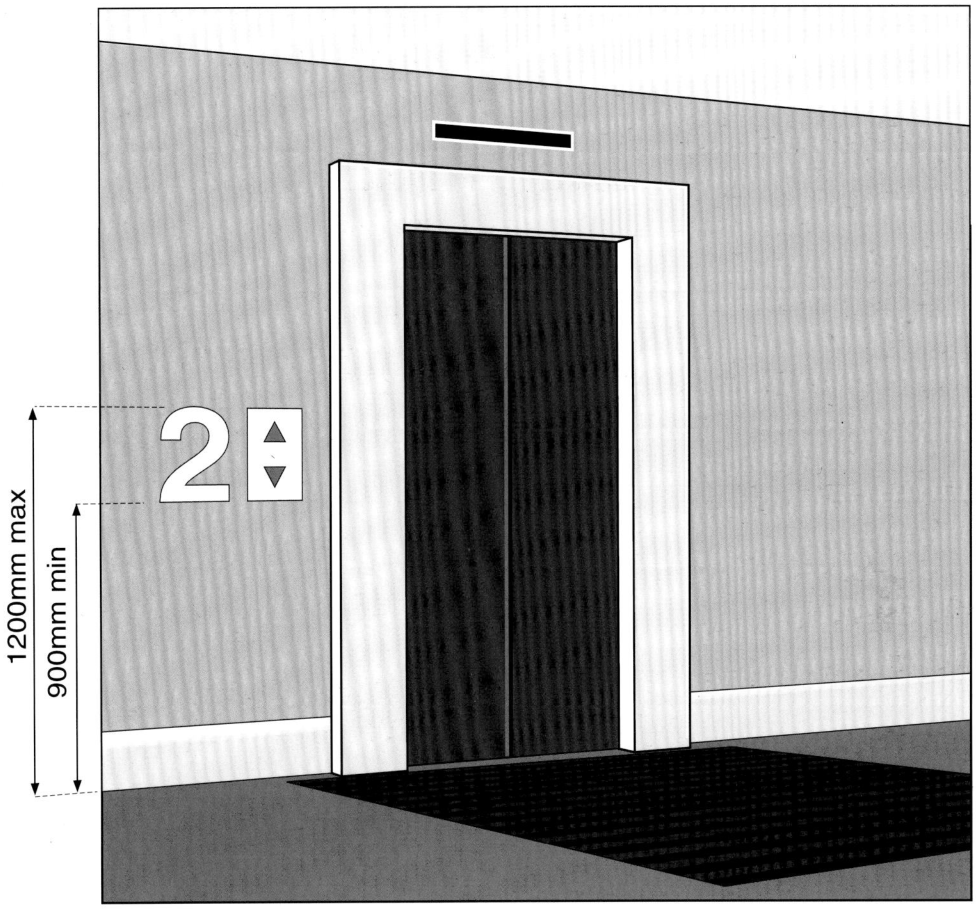

Horizontal lift buttons are good for wheelchair users and Braille readers

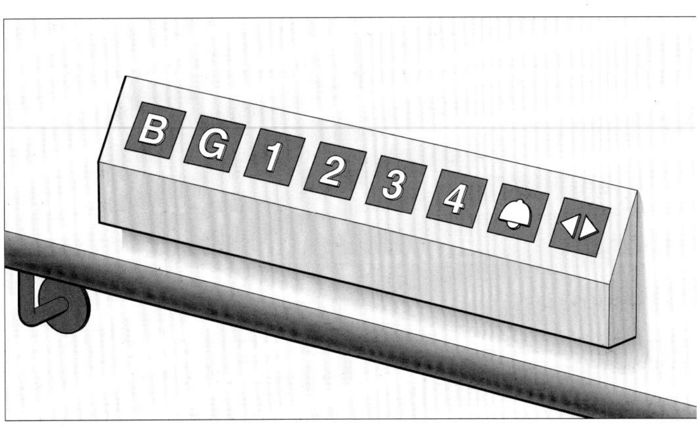

Lift – plan view

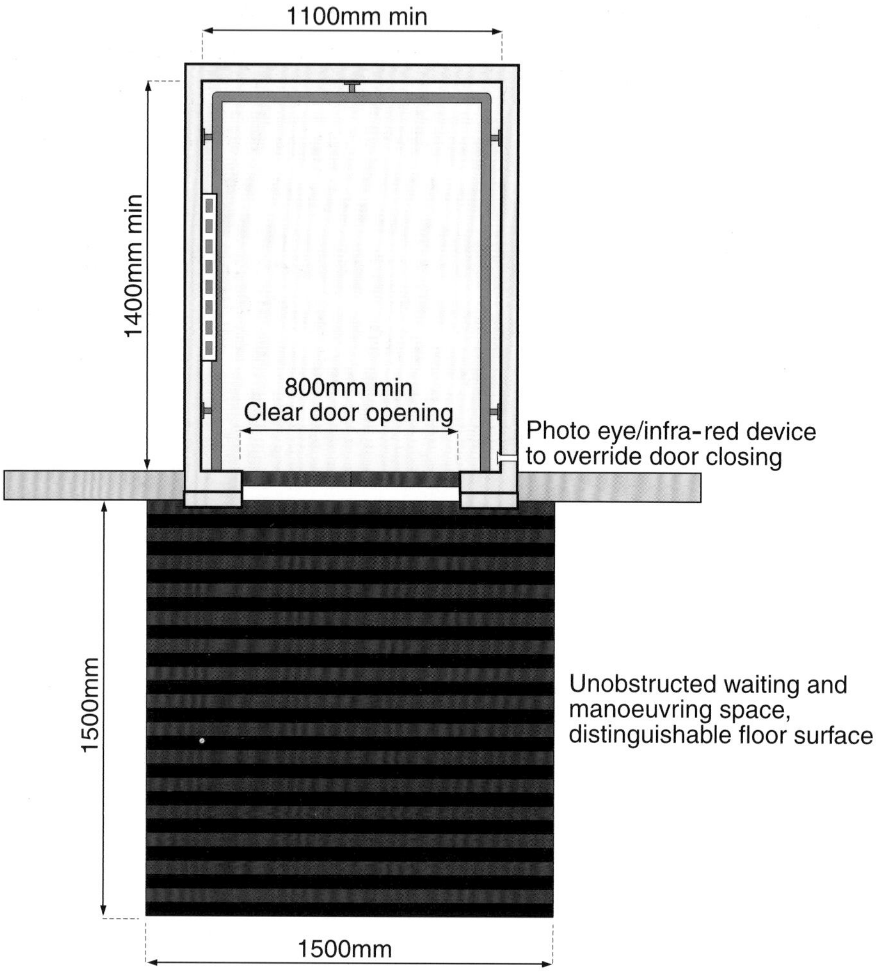

Lift – side view

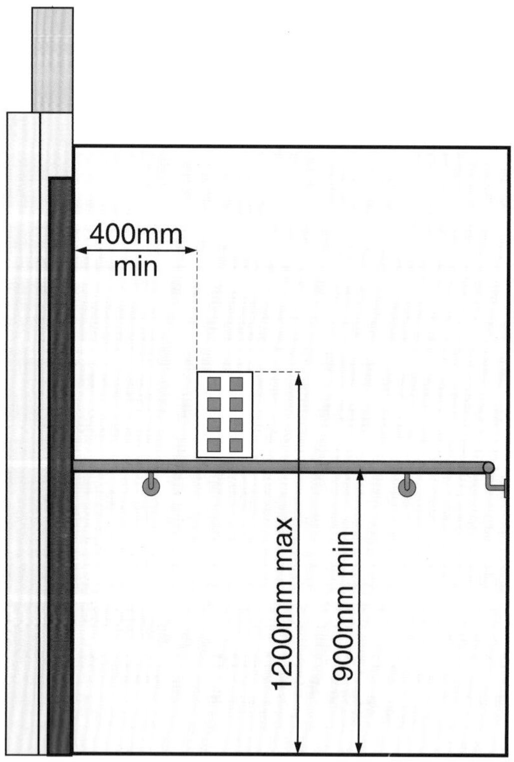

Other building controls

Door entry systems

Door entry systems using keypads should conform to the standard telephone keypad layout. There should always be a raised pip on the 5 button to allow people to calculate the relative positions of the other buttons.

Heating and ventilating controls

The conventional flat symbols should be replaced by embossed and colour-contrasted symbols.

3

Sign practicalities

3.1

Illumination and glare

Adequate lighting is especially important for most visually impaired and older people who generally require higher levels of illumination to read text. However, some people may be very sensitive to increased levels of illumination. Most lighting is designed to illuminate horizontal planes such as floors and desks, but signs are nearly always mounted vertically so additional measures may be needed to ensure adequate illumination.

Glare

Glare from lighting can be a major cause of discomfort in buildings. Glare occurs when one part of an interior is much brighter than the surrounding area. The most common causes of glare are from the following sources:

- luminaires and windows seen directly or indirectly
- indirect glare from a signboard with a high gloss finish
- direct glare from an internally illuminated sign

To minimise glare:

- use materials with a matt finish
- do not place suspended signs against a light source, eg. at the end of corridors which have windows or glass doors or against overhead light fittings
- do not position signs directly on to external glazing

If the existing lighting system is inadequate, localised lighting of the signs may be necessary, but internally illuminated signs are not recommended. If possible, all light sources should be concealed or shaded.

Colour rendering

The way we perceive colour is affected by the quality of the light source. Full spectrum lighting, as in clear daylight, is the most commonly acceptable. Colours can appear different under other light sources so, to avoid ineffective colour contrasts, it is always advisable to select colours under the lighting being used in the building.

3.2

Positioning

Signs to be read at close range

The average eye line of a person is in the range of 1400-1700mm above finished floor level. Signs, such as directories or identification signs on doors, that are intended to be read at close range, should be mounted as close to this as possible.

Signs to be read at medium range

Overhanging and projecting signs must be positioned high enough to avoid causing an obstruction. 2300mm to the underside is the recommended dimension from finished floor level. Flat-fixed wall-mounted signs should be placed high enough so as not to be obscured by people congregating nearby and should project no more than 100mm.

Signs to be read at long range

Long range signs are best positioned at a height that renders the signs obvious and avoids them being obscured by intervening objects such as cars.

Signs with a control element

Where signs are accompanied by a control panel they should be positioned within easy reach. The range 900-1200mm above finished floor level meets the needs of those sitting in a wheelchair as well as those standing.

Braille and embossed signs

Mounting locations for Braille and embossed signs should allow a person to approach and touch the message with ease. Users should not encounter protruding objects or have to stand within the swing of a door.

Braille and embossed room identification signs should be placed on the wall beside the latch side of the door, except for toilet and washroom doors. In the UK it is more usual to find toilet signs mounted on the door. The reasons for wall-mounting are:

- because doors are often left open
- to prevent the door being opened from the inside whilst someone is reading the sign by touch.

3.3

Organising a sign system

Once the detailed design guidance concerning the message (see section 2) and the sign itself (see section 3) has been applied to the outline information accumulated through the application of the planning process (see section 1), it is possible to draw up a detailed sign schedule for discussion with a sign manufacturer.

Planning a visual route

- begin as early as possible. Walk round and assess where signs may be needed. Do not forget directories and plans

- take a set of floor plans with you and check the location of each sign, then give it a unique number

- use a printed sign schedule form to write out the text of each sign in rough. If possible, take photographs for the positioning of directories, plans and room identification signs

- establish the functions of the site – alighting point, access, transfer, infrastructure. The distance between the starting point and the destination points should be by the shortest and most convenient routes. Do not forget the return to the reception area and the way out

- look at junctions, crossover points and main decision points (ie. where do I go now?); they will need extra signs. Where long distances are involved, repeat signs at regular intervals for reassurance. Do not forget floor numbers near lifts and in stairwells on each floor. If suspended signs are to be used, consider the addition of wall-mounted signs including Braille and embossed text

- Decide where symbols could be helpful and appropriate

- Check heights, visibility and fixing on site with your sign contractor or consultant and keep them in consistent positions throughout the building. Check that there is adequate wall space available. Remember to avoid placing signs where there could be glare.

Specific sign requirements

Determine as you go round each area what signs may be required. There is no mystique about this. It is usually common sense, but a rough sketch of each sign can be very useful.

After the site survey, the schedule can be written in full and a list of sign types allocated. If required, the sign contractor or consultant would prepare this section from your sketches and would then produce dimensioned drawings in colour for consideration and final checking, before production.

3.4

Maintenance

To keep signs in good condition and legible, a regular programme of cleaning and maintenance should be adopted. The frequency of cleaning will depend on the location, usage and climate; external signs in winter may need to be cleaned on a weekly basis, whilst internal signs in offices may need cleaning only occasionally.

Good maintenance will include not only cleaning, but physical repair to the sign if it becomes necessary. It should be acknowledged that Braille and embossed signs receive, by their nature, much handling and may require more cleaning than a complementary visual sign.

All good signmakers should be able to offer specific advice and help with sign maintenance.

3.5

Alterations

The sign requirements of most organisations change frequently; departments are re-named, people leave or move offices, routes are altered or changing safety regulations require modification. People lose confidence when information is inaccurate or out-of-date and it is important that, whatever changes are made, they should be in the same style, size and finish as the existing signs.

If maintaining a signing system within a company, one individual or department should be made responsible for all signs and should be aware of the standards and specification required. This information should be documented so that new or replacement signs can be ordered, when required, to match the existing signing system.

Consider either preparing a reference manual of signs in-house or requesting a sign manual from the sign contractor or consultant. The manual should include sign types, colours, type styles, sizes, locations, contact information etc. For very large schemes, or those on which information changes regularly, systematic audits should be carried out at regular intervals.

Care should be taken when selecting a sign system that it is adaptable to future site changes. If departments move or individuals change offices, an interchangeable sign (where slats can be moved around) would be preferable to one which has to be completely replaced.

Where flexibility is required (eg. for name changes), a room identification sign that incorporates an embossed and Braille room number with a PC generated name insert can be invaluable. This system is also useful for temporary signs (eg. for conferences and events).

A good signing system is one that continues to look good six months after installation, without having hand-written notes stuck to obsolescent signs due to an direction or departmental change. The cheapest option is not always the best.

4.0

Appendices

4.1

Introducing JMU

JMU Access Partnership is a pan disability access consultancy, jointly supported by the Royal National Institute for the Blind and the Guide Dogs for the Blind Association.

JMU Access Partnership aims to help enable people with serious sight problems and other disabilities lead full and independent lives through improving access to the built environment. They do this through their consultancy, training, publications, research and policy activities.

Training and consultancy is delivered through a team of access consultants based in London, Leeds, Edinburgh and Cardiff. Consultants are drawn from the construction, design or research related professions.

Clients include architects, developers, local authorities and service providers, in fact all those engaged in managing or developing the built environment. JMU Access Partnership's three main fields of interest are buildings, transport and the street environment.

For new build schemes, they offer design appraisals, where they work as part of the design team offering solutions and advice as to how to make new schemes accessible for people with disabilities.

For existing properties, they offer access audits where they identify all barriers and hazards to mobility and make recommendations as to how these may be overcome.

JMU's training programme covers general design issues relating to disability access and the Disability Discrimination Act, as well as specific technical courses on the various aspects of inclusive design.

All JMU's advice is in line with current best practice, much of which they have been involved in developing. Whilst following their advice does not offer immunity from litigation under the Disability Discrimination Act, engaging an access consultant suggests that disability access issues are being taken seriously, and that a reasonable approach is being taken.

4.2

Introducing the Sign Design Society

The Sign Design Society was formed in 1991 to promote excellence in signing. Its membership is drawn from any and all of the various skills which contribute to this frequently underestimated, yet vitally important, discipline.

There are six main objectives:

- to provide discussion and greater understanding between professionals in the sign industry
- to provide a central source for consultation and reference
- to promote international standards for graphic communication
- to harmonise legislation affecting signing in Europe and throughout the world
- to establish codes of professional and ethical conduct for all engaged in the commission, design and manufacture of signs and the establishment of standards of manufacture and performance
- to lobby for the introduction of sign design in education curricula at all levels

Members also enjoy a programme of seminars and debates, a quarterly newsletter 'Directions', national awards and contacts with the sign industry.

4.3

Additional wayfinding devices and techniques

Aromas

Aromas can make external wayfinding easier whether through the use of aromatic wood, flowering plants, scented foliage or herbs. Combined with the tactile quality of some shrubs and trees, much could be done to make them useful as wayfinding aids.

Internally, areas can be designated through aroma whether they are washrooms, laundries, kitchens or coffee areas. Although it may be impractical to manipulate the positions of these activities on site, it is important to recognise that the clues they produce will aid orientation, particularly for visually impaired people who make use of an enhanced sense of smell.

A number of companies now produce machines that produce pleasant aromas. These have obvious usage in certain areas of buildings but could be used as wayfinding clues if some thought is given to aromas for specific locations.

Other sensory input

The movement of air and the temperature of the air currents can also give important clues as to what is going on in the environment. Kinaesthetic information derived from the faculty, which perceives voluntary motions of the body, can be as important as sounds and aromas. It can, for example, give important clues to the length and possibly the height of a space through the waft of air current experienced coming through a swing door.

Induction loops

Induction loops work by converting sound via a microphone into a varying magnetic field which is converted back to amplified sound by an individual's hearing aid. Loops help to cut out extraneous background noise.

Induction loops should be fitted wherever information is given verbally – airports, railway stations, box offices, ticket counters, banks, post offices, churches, meeting rooms, cinemas and theatres. Induction loops also allow sound to be picked up by hearing aid wearers in adjacent rooms; this is called overlap. This may be a problem in multi-screen cinemas or where confidentiality is required; in these cases infra-red systems may be more suitable.

Infra-red communication systems

Infra-red systems work on different principles to induction loops by converting a sound source into an infra-red light signal and require special receiving headsets.

This system is more suitable for controlled areas such as cinemas, theatres and lecture rooms where headsets can be borrowed from a central source. As the technology is based on light, sound cannot be picked up outside the room in which the infra-red signals are generated.

Smart cards

Self-service terminals are being used by the public for an increasing range of applications, but many people with various disabilities have difficulties in using such things as bank and cash dispensers, public telephones and card-controlled entry gates.

Smart card systems could easily be adapted to the requirements of special users if they were positioned with thought. For example, smart cards could be used a few metres from the terminal to alert a blind person with a verbal message or the terminal itself could become interactive.

Electronic travel aids

Whilst sighted people have access to a wide range of sources such as maps, guidebooks, timetables, advertisements etc, with which to plan their routes, the informational sources for those with visual disabilities are very restricted. Even on well-known routes travellers can find that changes in landmarks or new obstacles may cause disorientation and necessitate a new route. To keep them independently mobile, they need a mobile travel aid which will integrate information from the aid (which might be both directional and locational), the surrounding environment, and their memory.

Adaptation to public access technology

Automatic Teller Machines (ATMs).
Work has been carried out on how ATMs (cash dispenser machines) can be designed so that people with a wide range of impairments can easily use them. This has resulted in a specification document, covering the design of the ATM, its positioning and other issues which can then be used when specifying which ATMs should be installed and where they should be located.

Other machines

Information is available on the design, installation and use of all public access machines ranging from ticket machines to hand dryers so that they can be used by people with a wide range of disabilities.

Issues covered include the colour and font of any display, the height the machine is to be positioned, the type of ticket release and the wording of instructions.

4.4

JMU testing procedures

Testing procedures

The recommendations in this publication are based on research drawn together from a number of diverse situations and evaluation projects.

Principal among those are the ones listed below:

JMU Evaluation Project 1997-8

A range of samples were evaluated by a wide cross section of visually impaired people. The variables were:

- character height
- character spacing (letter to letter and word to word)

For Braille: bold, medium and fine letterforms were evaluated with a cross section of profiles – rectangular with either square, chamfered, or rounded edges (including half round profile), upper and lower case variants and various depths of embossing

The users were a cross section of males and females, aged from 20 to 65 and above. Most were visually impaired later in life and were not Braille users.

Some users were residents of sheltered accommodation, others were more mobile and were users of public access buildings and public transport.

Interviews were carried out either in their home environment or local community centres. There was a wide geographical spread throughout the UK.

In addition, research has been studied from other countries:

Germany

'Improving visual information in public places' (Federal Ministry of Health, Bonn, 1996).

This evaluation was carried out in Germany over a period of three years and involved many organisations of users within Germany.

USA

The 'Americans with Disabilities Act' introduced specifications for visual and embossed signs, which have been in use now since 1991.

Canada

CNIB, Eyecatch and the Canadian Government have carried out comprehensive research into visual and embossed signs; specifications have been introduced through legislation and good practice guides.

Evaluation has revealed divided opinions on the use of upper case or lower case letters. It seems to depend largely on the educational background of individuals. Those who lose their sight later in life are able to understand both upper and lower case letters with relative ease. Those whose education is based on Braille only, prefer upper case letters. It is anticipated that, as more visually impaired children enter mainstream education, there will be a wider acceptance of both upper and lower case.

For combination signs, that is those that need to provide good legibility and tactile properties, upper and lower case should be used.

Summary

Information drawn from the above sources, has been the foundation for the specifications in this publication.

The research undertaken has shown common results in most cases. The main difference has been in the depth of embossing. The 'Americans with Disabilities Act' standard of 0.72mm has been found insufficient in practice, hence the minimum recommendation in this publication of 1mm.

4.5

Products and processes

Within the sign industry there are a vast number of materials, processes and techniques for producing signs: from printed paper, costing a few pence, to polished, halo illuminated stainless steel signs, costing thousands of pounds.

The types of sign chosen will depend on a number of factors; style, existing architecture, identity, sign supplier and, of course, cost.

When it comes to Braille and embossed signs, maps, plans and diagrams, however, the choice is a little more limited although varied all the same. Due to the nature of the signs and how they will be used, it is vital that they conform to a set of design standards and specifications.

The use of embossed text, rather than engraved text, will greatly improve legibility. Embossing text to a minimum of 1mm and a maximum of 1.5mm with no sharp edges etc., ensures that maximum legibility is achieved. Whether the sign is made from wood, plastic, metal or stone, its legibility will not be affected, providing the design specifications have been followed.

Braille is probably one of the most difficult parts of a sign to produce both accurately and legibly. A Braille cell consists of a number of dots to create a recognisable character; it never changes in size and each individual dot has to have exactly the same domed shape as the previous one. The ideal dot is a 1.4mm diameter sphere set just over half of its depth into the surface of the sign. Spacing is also crucial both dot to dot and inter-character (see section 2.3).

There are a number of processes and materials available to produce an acceptable Braille and embossed sign.

As technology develops, the number of processes available to produce suitable, cost-effective Braille and embossed signs, maps, plans and diagrams will increase. Some of the processes currently available include:

- plastic signs using cut out characters and glass, plastic, resin or metal Braille

- a 3M process involving building up the characters and Braille and then covering the sign in a clear, heat-applied film

- photopolymers using a printing technique to produce both characters and Braille

- sand blasting timber, glass and other suitable materials

- engraving away the surplus material to leave the character and Braille raised

- acid etching to remove the surplus material

- casting in metal to produce characters and models

- vacuum forming for the production of maps and diagrams

- Minolta paper, sometimes called swell paper, for making Braille, characters, maps and diagrams.

The above processes are all able to produce acceptable results and may be used in combination with each other, if required.

4.6

Materials and finishes chart

Chart headings	Finish
Painted aluminium / steel / enamelled and vitreous surfaces	Use matt finish paints
Anodised aluminium	Usually a matt finish
Foam PVC	Supplied in non-reflective finishes as standard
Painted MDF	Use matt finish paint
Acrylic sheet	Specify non-reflective finish
GRP	Specify non-reflective finish
Vinyl, either as self-adhesive or applied to another material	Use matt finish

Avoid polished surfaces eg:	natural polished wood
	brass
	satin finish stainless steel

4.7

ISO and BSI Standards

- **Public Information Symbols** BS 6034: 1990 ISO 7001: 1990

- **Safety signs and colours** BS 5378
  Part 1: Specification for colour and design
  Part 2: Specification for calorimetric and photometric properties of materials
  Part 3: Specification for additional signs to those given in BS 5378: Part 1

- **Fire safety signs, notices and graphic symbols** BS 5499
  Part 1: Specification for fire safety signs
  Part 2: Specification for self-luminous fire safety signs
  Part 3: Specification for internally-illuminated fire safety signs

- **Fire precautions in the design and construction of buildings** BS 5588
  Part 8: Code of practice for means of escape for disabled people

  Available from BSI Customer Services, 389 Chiswick High Road, London W4 4AL

- **Health & Safety (Safety Signs and Signals) Regulations 1996** 92/58/EEC
  Available from HSE Books, PO Box 1999, Sudbury, Suffolk CO10 2WA

- **EC Safety Signs Directive 1996** 92/58/EEC
  Available from The Stationery Office, Scanfax Department, 51 Nine Elms Lane, London SW8 5DR

- **Building Regulations 1991 Part 1 – Access and Facilities for Disabled People – Approved Document M**
  ISBN 0 11 753469 2
  Available from The Stationery Office, The Publications Centre, PO Box 276, London SW8 5DT

4.8 Useful addresses

JMU Access Partnership
224 Great Portland Street
London W1N 6AA
Tel: 020 7391 2002
email: jmu@rnib.org.uk
website: www.jmuaccess.org.uk

Sign Design Society
66 Derwent Road
Kinsbourne Green
Harpenden
Herts AL5 3NX
Tel: 01582 713556
email: enquiries@signdesignsociety.co.uk
website: www.signdesignsociety.co.uk

Nova Polymers
27 Holywell Road
London EC2A 4JB
Tel: 020 7377 0191
Fax: 020 7377 2431
email: sales@novapolymers.co.uk
website: www.novapolymers.co.uk

The Access Association
Walsall MBC
Civic Centre, Darwell Street
Walsall WS1 1TP
Tel/Text: 01922 652010
email: FoxS@Walsall.gov.uk

British Sign Association
5 Orton Enterprise Centre
Bakewell Road
Orton, Southgate
Peterborough PE2 6XU
Tel: 01733 230033
email: bsa@sign.u-net.com
website: www.british-sign-assoc.co.uk

BSI Standards
389 Chiswick High Road
London W4 4AL
Tel: 020 8996 9001
email: info@bsi.org.uk
website: www.bsi.org.uk

Centre for Accessible Environments
Nutmeg House
60 Gainsford Street
London SE1N 2NY
Tel: 020 7357 8182
email: info@cae.org.uk
website: www.cae.org.uk

Chartered Society of Designers (CSD)
First Floor
32/38 Saffron Hill
London EC1N 8FH
Tel: 020 7831 9777
email: csd@csd.org.uk

Guide Dogs for the Blind Association
Hillfields
Burghfield Common
Reading RG7 3YG
Berkshire
Tel: 0118 983 5555
email: guidedogs@gdba.org.uk
website: www.gdba.org.uk

RADAR
12 City Forum
250 City Road
London EC1 8AF
Tel: 020 7250 3222
Minicom 020 7250 4119
email: radar@radar.org.uk
website: www.radar.org.uk

Royal Institute of British Architects (RIBA)
66 Portland Place
London W1 W1N 4AD
Tel: 020 7580 5533
email: admin@inst.riba.org
website: www.architecture.com

Royal National Institute for the Blind (RNIB)
224 Great Portland Street
London W1N 4AD
Tel: 020 7388 1266
website: www.rnib.org.uk

RNIB Speaking Sign
(ref: DH124, DH130, DH140)
Royal National Institute for the Blind, PO Box 173
Peterborough PE2 6WS
Tel: 0345 023 153
email: cservices@rnib.org.uk

Push and Talk audible signs (extra heavy duty use)
Horizon Marketing Ltd.
Unit 15B, Home Mills Industrial Park
Britannia Road
Huddersfield HD3 4QF
Tel: 01484 460909
email: sales@horizonsigns.fsbusiness.co.uk
website: www.horizon-signs.com

Royal Institute of Chartered Surveyors (RICS)
12 Great George Street
Parliament Square
London SW1P 3AD
Tel: 020 7222 7000
website: www.rics.org

The UK Association of Braille Producers
exists to make Braille more readily available.
It provides a forum for information and advice and can be contacted at:
Royal National Institute for the Blind (RNIB)
PO Box 173
Peterborough PE2 6WS
email: cservices@rnib.org.uk
website: www.rnib.org.uk

For information on audible signs please contact:
JMU Access Partnership
(address on page 86)

For information on the colour palette please contact:
JMU Access Partnership
(address on page 86)

For information on sign designers please contact:
Chartered Society of Designers (address on page 88)
Sign Design Society (address on page 87)

4.9

Bibliography

Alternative Highway Sign Alphabet for Older Drivers
Carol Tan
Texas A&M University, College Station, TX
USA 1991

Building Sight
Barker, Barrick, Wilson. RNIB 1995

Barrier Free Design
James Holmes-Siedle, Butterworth Architecture, London 1996

Colour, Contrast and Perception
Bright, Cook, Harris. Reading University 1997

Colour and Contrast
Dulux Technical Group, ICI plc. 1997

Disability Discrimination Act, 1995
Department for Education and Employment, plus relevant Codes of Practice

Disability in Great Britain
DSS 1999

Improving Visual Information in Public Places
Federal Ministry of Health, Bonn 1996

NHS Wayfinding, Guidance for Healthcare Facilities
NHS Estates 1999

Orientation and Wayfinding in Public Buildings
Public Works, Canada 1988

The Americans with Disabilities Act
US Department of Justice, Washington 1991

4.10

Glossary of terms

Ascender	A part of a letter that extends above the main part
Braille cell	Area that contains a Braille letter
Chamfered	A bevelled surface at an edge or corner
Descender	A part of a letter that descends below the line
Embossed	Term applied to symbols or lettering which stand proud of the surface
Engraved	Inscribe or cut on a hard surface
Fugitive	Term applied to colour which fades in sunlight or bright light
Gloss	Surface shine
Halation	Spreading of light beyond its proper extent; effect which happens if too much contrast is used
Hue	Term for the quality of a colour which distinguishes one colour from another eg. red, green, blue etc.
Kinaesthetic	The brain's awareness of the position of the body or limbs
Locator	A semi-circular raised, or recessed, indicator to identify the location of Braille
Lower case	Without capital letters
Macular	A small part at the centre of the back of the eye where incoming rays are focussed. It is used for fine detail and colour vision.
Matt	Dull surface as opposed to gloss surface

Overlap	To partly cover another object or sound
Sans serif	Without projections to the ends of letters
Serif	Slight projection which finishes the stroke of a letter
Swell paper	A specialised paper that can be used to create embossed characters through a heat process
Symbol	Pictorial representation of an idea
Tone	The tint or shade of a colour
Upper case	Capital letters only
Wayfinding	Means of finding a route around a building or site

4.11

About the authors

Peter Barker OBE, BSc(Eng), DMS, FBIM, MCILT worked in manufacturing for many years and was then a Director of various companies in the building and construction industry.

Being visually impaired, he brought his own personal experience and wider knowledge to RNIB in 1991 to set up the RNIB/GDBA Joint Mobility Unit (JMU). He joined the Sign Design Society when it was formed and is now a member of its management group. He has worked with a number of sign manufacturing companies in the UK and abroad and with various research organisations, in order to develop standards for design.

More recently, Peter has been in much demand as a speaker and travels extensively to talk about the improvements that can be made to make the physical environment more accessible. Peter was awarded the OBE in 2000 for his services to the mobility of disabled people.

June Fraser ARCA PPCSD MInst Pkg graduated from the Royal College of Art in 1957. Her first job was with Design Research Unit (Architects & Designers). In 1980, she moved to the John Lewis Partnership as Head of Graphic Design. In 1984 she joined The Design Council as Head of the Industrial Design Division and, since 1988, she has been in private practice.

Her first contact with Peter Barker was on 'Building Sight' which she was asked to design and produce; this led on to the 'Sign Design Guide'. She is also involved with the British Standards Institute on symbols and signs for people with special needs.

From 1983-85 she was President of the CSD (Chartered Society of Designers) and from 1989-1993 on the Board of ICSID (International Council for Societies of Industrial Design). Currently, she is a Member of Court at the Royal College of Art, a Governor of KIAD (The Kent Institute of Art & Design) and of Talbot Heath, her old school. She is a director of the Sign Design Society and was Chairman from 1995-97.